LILI'UOKALANI

LILIʻUOKALANI

Aldyth Morris

UNIVERSITY OF HAWAII PRESS
HONOLULU

Printed in the United States of America

98 97 96 95 94 93 5 4 3 2 1

Library of Congress Cataloging-in-Publication Data

Morris, Aldyth, 1901–
    Lili'uokalani / Aldyth Morris.
      p.   cm.
    ISBN 0-8248-1543-2
    1. Liliuokalani, Queen of Hawaii, 1838–1917—Drama.
    2. Hawaii—History—To 1893—Drama.   I. Title.
PS3563.O87397L55 1993
812'.54–dc20   93-3717
                                       CIP

Front cover: Lili'uokalani, 1913. (Photo by Bonnie.
Hawaii State Archives.)
Frontispiece: Portrait of Queen Lili'uokalani by
William Cogswell. (The Friends of 'Iolani Palace.)

University of Hawaii Press books are printed
on acid-free paper and meet the guide-
lines for permanence and durability of the
Council on Library Resources

Designed by Paula Newcomb

To Dix and Jan

THE CAST

QUEEN LILIʻUOKALANI: Leo Anderson Akana
KALA: Victoria Nalani Kneubuhl

Liliʻuokalani received its world premiere presentation by Manoa
Valley Theatre, Honolulu, Hawaiʻi, on 1 July 1992. The production
was directed by Robert T. Stach; the set design was by Paul Gun-
cheon; lighting design was by Sandy Sandelin; and costume design
was by Sandra Finney.

in its 23rd season
presents

KE KALAUNU, ME KA LEI (Crown and Wreath)
Quilt made ca. 1900, cotton, yellow on red.
Collection of Daughters of Hawaii.

Liliʻuokalani

by Aldyth Morris

July 1 - 26, 1992

Underwritten by **First Hawaiian Bank**

MANOA VALLEY THEATRE
Honolulu's off-Broadway, 150-seat playhouse

ACKNOWLEDGMENTS

A number of people have given generously of time and talent during the writing of *Lili'uokalani*. I wish to acknowledge contributions and offer my heartfelt thanks to the following:

My son, Richard V. Morris, for his critical support and for the endless electronic versions of the play; his wife, Janice Morris, for patient assistance with the proofreading; the State Foundation on Culture and the Arts for their financial grant; Tomi Knaefler, Jean King, and Mason Altiery for their insights and suggestions and enduring patience as they listened to the rewrites; Eugene Lyon for the suggestion that I write the play, and to his daughter Jen, who shared with me some of her own research about the Queen; Linda Ryan for her continuing interest in the play; Kekuni Blaisdell, for encouragement and information that only one of Hawaiian blood could provide; Dorothy Gillett for sharing her knowledge about the Queen's musical compositions; James Wright for legal advice and a casual remark that led to certain revisions of the play; Dwight Martin and the Manoa Valley Theatre for giving the play its premiere performance; Bob Stach for his critical evaluation of the script and pertinent suggestions; Iris Wiley for her enthusiastic invitation to submit the manuscript to the University of Hawaii Press; Scott Spallina for the many trips to the post office, library, and copying machines on my behalf; and, most particularly, all the Hawaiian people who, during the sixty-three years of my residence in Hawai'i, talked freely with me about their beloved Queen.

CHRONOLOGY

SEPTEMBER 2	1838	Lydia Lili'u Loloku Walania Wewehi Kamaka'eha is born to Kapa'akea and Keohokalole. She is immediately taken to be raised by Konia, granddaughter of Kamehameha I, and High Chief Paki.
JUNE	1842	Enrolled as a boarder in the Chiefs' Children's School. Leaves in 1848 but continues schooling under a tutor.
	1860	Becomes engaged to John Owen Dominis, son of an American sea captain who has built a home in Honolulu.
SEPTEMBER 16	1862	Marries John O. Dominis and goes to live in Washington Place.
	1866	At the request of King Kamehameha V, she composes an anthem for her people, *"He Mele Lāhui Hawai'i."*
FEBRUARY 12	1874	Her brother David Kalākaua is elected King.
APRIL 10	1877	She is named heir apparent and becomes Princess Lili'uokalani.

July 6	1887	A small group of businessmen, most of foreign parentage, force the King to sign a new constitution that significantly reduces the power of the throne. Lili'uokalani labels it the Bayonet Constitution because it was "forced" on the King.
January 20	1891	King Kalākaua dies in San Francisco.
January 29	1891	Lili'uokalani is proclaimed Queen.
August 27	1891	John O. Dominis dies.
January 14	1893	Queen announces her plan to proclaim a new constitution but is persuaded to postpone it. The opposition, principally foreigners, plots a revolution.
January 16	1893	From a warship anchored in Honolulu Harbor, American armed military forces are landed "to protect American life and property," but they take up positions threatening to the Queen's forces.
January 17	1893	On the steps of an almost empty government building, a revolutionary group reads a proclamation abrogating the monarchy and establishing a provisional government until terms of annexation have been arranged with the United States.
January 17	1893	American Minister John L. Stevens recognizes the provisional government. The Queen, under protest, yields her authority, not to the provisional government but to

the United States until such time as it, upon the facts having been presented, shall undo the actions of its representative and restore Lili'uokalani to her throne.

JANUARY 18	1893	Commissioners representing the provisional government charter a boat and depart for Washington, D.C., to tell their story of the overthrow. The Queen's representative is denied passage on the boat.
FEBRUARY 3	1893	Representatives of provisional government arrive in Washington.
FEBRUARY 14	1893	Annexation treaty has been signed by President Benjamin Harrison.
FEBRUARY 15	1893	President Harrison sends the treaty to the Senate.
MARCH 9	1893	President-elect Grover Cleveland withdraws it from the Senate and decides to inquire into the circumstances of the revolution.
MARCH 29	1893	Commissioner James H. Blount arrives to investigate.
AUGUST 9	1893	Blount departs for Washington with a "formidable amount of testimony."
NOVEMBER 4	1893	Congressman Albert B. Willis arrives in Honolulu with a message for the Queen.
DECEMBER 18	1893	Queen grants full amnesty to those involved in the revolution.

JULY 7	1898	Newlands Resolution has passed both houses of Congress, and President McKinley signs it into law.
AUGUST 2	1898	Liliʻuokalani returns to Hawaiʻi.
AUGUST 12	1898	Annexation ceremonies at the Palace. Queen remains secluded in Washington Place as the Hawaiian flag comes down and the American flag is raised above the Palace.

Act One

(The curtain is always up. House and stage lights are down. A chant extolling the deeds of LILIʻUOKALANI's *ancestors is heard. As the chant comes to an end the stage lights begin to come up very slowly)*

KALA: *(To the audience)* Aloha kākou.

When I awoke this morning to cloudy skies and bits of rain, when I contemplated the ceremonies to take place this morning on the Palace steps, I thought of Kitty— Eveline Townsend Wilson, that is. Kitty and I were ladies-in-waiting to the Queen and were with her through many of her trials—her imprisonment, for instance. On this particular day we would have come together to Washington Place to assure Her Majesty of our love and loyalty. But since Kitty is no longer with us I have come alone. My name is Kala.

Her Majesty received me warmly, but naturally she was preoccupied, so I didn't delay my leaving. I did tell her, however, that although I had a ticket to a seat on the upper balcony which was reserved for the public, I didn't plan to attend the ceremonies. The Queen herself will be inside, with doors and windows closed and curtains drawn. But when she said that if I wished I could watch the flag-raising ceremonies from right here on her *lānai*, I accepted her suggestion gladly. I can see almost everything. Excuse me—

They've just thrown open the rear door of the Palace and I can see straight through to the huge platform the P.G.s—we still call them the P.G.s—have erected

1

over the front steps of the Palace. The platform itself is decorated with flags and bunting—red, white, and blue bunting—and someone is rearranging the chairs. Chairs for the "important personages" invited to today's ceremonies, the paper says.

Which reminds me. On the chance that Her Majesty had not seen last night's paper, I drew her attention to the editor's remarks. (*Quoting*) "No one with any sense expects members of the royal family to come to watch their flag hauled down forever. But not to honor them with an invitation would be an insult."

(The lights are up now. The QUEEN *is seen standing, newspaper in hand, reading the editor's remarks. Her words overlap what* KALA *is saying)*

LILI'UOKALANI: (*Reading*)—to watch their flag hauled down forever. But not to honor them with an invitation would be an insult. (*To herself*) An insult? After so many, does one more matter? But the editor is right. My reserved seat on the platform will be empty. I've seen our flag hauled down before—

(Coming downstage and speaking to the audience)

—when I was a child. At a meeting in the Fort downtown. We pupils of the Chiefs' Children's School are there by invitation. I am small and can see nothing but the legs around me. Bare brown legs, trousered legs of businessmen and missionaries, uniformed legs of ships' officers and police, and way up high, above the crowd, our flag.

Suddenly a voice cries out, "Hear ye! Hear ye!" and all legs turn in one direction. Then the King's voice: "I am in perplexity, my people. Perplexity not of my own making. I am being forced to cede our islands to Great Britain. If I refuse, a British ship in harbor will shell the islands and we may all be killed. I cede our islands under protest for I believe that Queen Victoria, when she learns the truth, will restore to us our sovereignty."

(Punchbowl guns)

There is a deafening gun salute, and when I open my eyes and look again our flag is gone. As the British flag is raised their ship's band plays "Isle of Beauty, Fare Thee Well." And Mrs. Cooke said she saw the King close his eyes and let the tears roll unheeded down his cheeks.

My older brother, David Kalākaua, tears the gold insignia from his cap and tramples it in the dust. The other boys do the same. "We are no longer chiefs," they cry. *"Auwē, auwē."*

Soon all Hawaiian flags are confiscated—even the little ones we have at school.

(Music, "God Save the Queen")

For five long months we're British subjects. Captain Paulet and his redcoats—"lobsterbacks" we children call them—come swaggering down the street, ordering us about, coming late to Sunday services in the Stone Church, and sitting anywhere they like—even in the royal pew.

Then one day another British ship arrives, bringing Admiral Richard Thomas and more redcoats. With their ship's band playing "God Save the Queen," they march up King Street, and the admiral seeks an audience with the King. Next day, the King walks in procession with the chiefs to the Stone Church. Admiral

Thomas's message is read to the whole town assembled there.

"Queen Victoria repudiates the actions of Captain Paulet. She acknowledges you, King Kamehameha Third, the rightful ruler of the Hawaiian islands."

The King, tears streaming down his face, proclaims, *"Ua mau ke ea o ka 'āina i ka pono."* The life of the land is preserved in righteousness.

(Choir sings "The Restoration Anthem")

To the tune of "God Save the Queen," the ladies sing "The Restoration Anthem," with the gallant Admiral Thomas joining in. There is a pageant in the pasture-lands, and with Captain Paulet and his lobsterbacks to do the honors, the British flag comes down—

(Punchbowl guns)

—and our flag climbs the pole once more, to take its rightful place. For one breathless moment it hangs limp, then a gentle breeze unfurls it there against the sky for all the world to see. And nothing, nothing in my young life has seemed so beautiful. Then we, the children of the chiefs, march through the city, singing "The Restoration Anthem," each holding high a sweet potato with a small Hawaiian flag stuck in it. The King proclaims a ten-day holiday and releases all the prisoners in the Fort.

The next day Admiral Thomas pays a visit to our school. He takes particular note of Alexander Liholiho, heir apparent to the throne, gives him a pair of epaulets to wear. He takes note of me, too. Asks my name. When I tell him it's Lydia, Mrs. Cooke says, "She is a child of chiefs. She may one day be Queen. If she lives, that is."

If she lives—what does that mean? It's not long before I understand.

(The hollow sound of wagons is heard. A funeral chant begins)

I can still hear the wagons rattling through deserted streets; yellow wagons, collecting the bodies of the dead. I can still see the coffins, hundreds of them, then three special coffins, two resting on the ground, a smaller one on top. The smaller coffin holds the body of my baby sister, only recently adopted by the King. Three of Hawai'i's future chiefs are dead in one day—of measles. Of the babies born during this epidemic, not one survives.

I know now—the farewell chant, the wail and lament, the devastating, paralyzing grief that followed the three coffins to their graves was not for them alone. Not even for the eleven thousand recent dead of measles. Not even for the living bodies of our people riddled with what the sailors call the pox. The lament was for all Hawaiians—their virgin blood holds no immunity to the diseases that the stranger brings.

(An offstage noise is heard. LILI'UOKALANI *goes to the window and closes it tightly, to shut out the sound of the ceremonies)*

KALA: *(To the audience)* That angry voice you hear is Minister Cooper chastising a news reporter for intimating in his column that all gates to the Palace grounds would be closed today. That never was the intention. The Richards Street and the Palace Walk gates are open to the public. Only the King Street gate is closed—yes, there is a mounted sentinel posted—but the gate is

5

closed simply to reserve a clear way for the troops. Troops?

LILI'UOKALANI: *(To the audience)* As I said, my reserved seat on the platform will be empty. I shall be here, in this room in Washington Place. A room so full of memories I wonder they don't smother me. Memories of people and events leading slowly, surely to this day of days. Each spot and corner, each piece of furniture, a witness to some happening leading to this moment. And we, the Hawaiian people, powerless to stop them.

This chair, for instance, is where my brother, David Kalākaua, sat when he told me how he was forced to sign the Bayonet Constitution, making him nothing but a puppet King.

(Punchbowl guns)

I am standing here when the Punchbowl guns announce the passing of my brother Leleiohoku.

The minister of foreign affairs called me on this telephone to tell me the *Charleston* had been sighted—the yards cockbilled and the flag half-mast.

Here, in this corner because he wanted privacy, is where a certain "mission boy" sat when he proposed I betray my brother, the King.

This is where American Commissioner Blount was standing when he handed me the slanderous clippings from the *Star*, assuring me they did not originate in his office. Then he sat down here and asked the names of the revolutionaries, and I gave them to him, one by one.

Congressman Willis sat in this straight-back chair when I handed him my grant of amnesty for those who had acted in my overthrow.

I was standing here, beside my desk, when the deputy sheriff, waving a white paper, orders Mrs. Clark and me to come with him. And through that open door I see the people gathering to watch a Queen arrested.

That night this room is searched by soldiers looking for evidence against me, pulling walls apart, tearing at the furniture, until this lovely room is nothing but a shambles.

There are personal memories, too. I have accepted the fact that I am barren, I have accepted the private sorrow that I cannot bear my husband's child and the public sorrow that if ever I am Queen I cannot produce a royal heir. Then one day, here in this room, Dr. Trousseau tells me that Mary Purdy wishes me to know that she is pregnant with my husband's child. When it is born, at my request they bring him to me here, wrapped in soft white *tapa*. I crush him to my empty breasts and call him John 'Aimoku.

(Lullaby music)

This chair, brought from my Pālama home, is where I sang to sleep my three beloved *hānai* babies—Lydia, John 'Aimoku, and Kaipo.

This window—but why go on. As I said, my seat on the platform will be empty. I shall be here, in Washington Place, in this room so full of yesterdays—remembering.

(An angry voice is heard offstage)

KALA: *(To the audience)* That's Minister Cooper again telling the news reporter that the issuing of cards to the public for preferred seats on the balcony was merely to avoid unseemly hustling for seats. There was no favoritism involved, none whatsoever. First come, first served.

(Sounds of Beretania Street)

LILIʻUOKALANI: *(To the audience)* Remembering how when I was growing up I'd often walk by Washington Place, wondering what it was like inside. I knew it was built by an American sea captain, John Dominis, and that he'd brought his Boston-born wife and his small son to live in it. People said that on his next voyage to Asia he would buy magnificent furnishings for the new home. But Captain Dominis was lost at sea on his next voyage. The widow Dominis rented rooms in the large house to support herself and her child. After an American statesman, during his brief residence, displayed an American flag over his quarters, it came to be called Washington Place.

I meet the young John Dominis when we are in our twenties.

What am I like at twenty? Not pretty, as Emma Rooke. Not beautiful, as my *hānai* sister, Bernice Pauahi. My gift is music. Mrs. Cooke says I have perfect pitch. To compose and sing are as natural to me as breathing.

My companions are Hawaiian girls of chiefly rank. And missionary daughters. I dress as they do—bonnet, bodice, full skirt, and button shoes. Except for my complexion I am much the same as they are. Superficially, that is, since I am a child of tropic islands and another race. At times my whole being cries out for something only half-remembered. Sometimes it's only fish and *poi* instead of meat, potatoes, gravy. Sometimes it's for the company of the *kūpuna*—the old ones who remember what it was like before the strangers came. The oldest ones remember well, for they were there when strange ships, big as floating islands, appeared on the horizon. The ships came close and strange pale-faced creatures stepped ashore like gods. My people fell face down on the sand before them. As the *kūpuna* talk I seem almost to remember what it was like before the strangers came, when the women and the taro fields were fertile, when *tapa* sounds were heard throughout the land, and Kāne of the Living Water was watching over us.

Oh, don't misunderstand me. I love my Christian prayer book. I attend services in the Stone Church regularly. Eventually I direct the choir there. One Christmas morning I remember in particular. A new organ has been installed. I'm to play it. When everyone is settled in his pew, when the last rustle of a satin skirt has died away, I place my fingers on the keys.

(Sound of an organ playing a Christmas hymn)

As the first notes reach even the farthest corner of the church my heart's about to burst with joy. You see, Bernice and I—with fairs and concerts and bazaars—have raised the money to buy this organ—a Christmas present for the church.

That's what I am like at twenty—when I meet the young John Dominis. At a moonlight dancing party. On board a British ship in port. Prince Lot introduces us. I remember our first conversation—

(To John Dominis)

Of course I remember you, John Dominis. You used to climb the fat brick wall between your school and mine, and sit there watching the children of the chiefs at play. You made me—uncomfortable. Once I spoke to you unkindly. . . . You don't remember? . . . I said I didn't like being watched. I asked you to go elsewhere. . . . No, you didn't go away. You just sat there, smiling. . . . Do I what? . . . No, John Dominis. I don't want you now to go away. I want you to ask me for a dance. *(Waltz music)*

(To the audience)

And so we dance. And talk. And laugh. And stand there at the railing in the moonlight. Presently John asks if he may see me home.

The next time I see John is at Nānākuli. The new King, Alexander Liholiho—remember the boy Admiral Thomas gave the epaulets to—and his pretty wife, Queen Emma, are entertaining the royal party at a picnic. John, as Prince Lot's good friend, has been invited.

After a pleasant time of picnicking and swimming, as John and I are riding back to Honolulu, a careless rider forces his horse between John's horse and mine. John is thrown. Without a word John gets up, mounts his horse, sees me home, dismounts to see me to the door, remounts his horse, and rides away. He is so pale and silent I think he's cross with me—or, rather, cross because I'd seen him lose his seat.

Next day I learn they took him all but fainting from his horse. His leg is broken. While it is mending we fall in love. I think—yes I can bear to say it now—I think I was more in love than John was.

Naturally my brother David Kalākaua is concerned.

(To Kalākaua)

You don't need to remind me, David. . . . I know the marriage of a chiefess is a matter of concern. . . . I know John is a *haole*. I know he's an American. But he's Prince Lot's good friend. He's on his staff. He's practically a member of the royal party. . . . But, David, my chances of becoming Queen are so remote. With at least ten aspirants ahead of me, including you. And there's the little Prince—Prince Albert. Now that Queen Emma's borne a son, the Kamehameha line could go on forever. . . . Anyway, being John's wife won't make me any less a Queen. . . . David, I love John. If he asks me— No, he hasn't asked me yet. . . . Very well, we'll wait until he does. Yes, David. If ever I am destined to be Queen, I will be ready.

(To the audience)

It's two years before John and I become engaged. Two more before the marriage date is set. When the pre-wedding festivities are at their height—one week before we are to take our vows—

(Funeral chant)

—the four-year-old Prince Albert—heir apparent to the throne, darling of his parents' hearts, hope of the Kamehameha line, pride of the Hawaiian people—dies.

Our wedding is postponed two weeks in deference. But what's two weeks when the entire kingdom mourns? Not only for the little Prince, but for the future of Hawai'i. Besides the present King there's only one Kamehameha left—the King's older, bachelor brother, Prince Lot. Unless he marries and begets an heir, the Kamehameha line will end forever.

No one is blind to what that means. Hawai'i's life as an independent kingdom depends on the preservation of the monarchy. Any break in the succession is an invitation—not only to the foreign powers beyond our shores but to the very foreigners within our midst.

11

(*Commotion outside.* LILIʻUOKALANI *goes to the window again and pulls the curtains closed, as though to further shut out the sounds*)

KALA: (*To the audience*) The public is beginning to arrive—most of them on foot.

(*Wedding music*)

LILIʻUOKALANI: (*To the audience*) On a warm September day, in the home of Charles and Bernice Pauahi Bishop, John and I are married by the Reverend Mr. Damon. And I am happy. Even the refusal of John's mother to attend the wedding does not dismay me.

After the ceremony John brings me here—to Washington Place—a bride. Mrs. Dominis—John's mother, that is—remains upstairs while John shows me the house. As I follow him from room to room, then to the little cottage in the rear where he and I will live, I face the chilling fact that this is not my home. I am a guest—a favored guest perhaps—but still a guest in someone else's home. To Mrs. Dominis, I, as her son's wife, am an intruder.

Of course, I want John's mother to like me. I cater to her wishes to an extent consistent with my personal dignity—sometimes far beyond. Even acceding later to her wish that I set up separate quarters elsewhere, leaving Washington Place to her and John once more. I am not completely banished. That would be a scandal. I have my room here—but when I am with John, I feel I am a visitor. When he comes to see me, he is my visitor. Sometimes, we sit together in his carriage for half an hour or so. Then he goes his way, and I go mine. As I told him once, I have a husband, but no one to wake up

12

to. Eventually, I do come back to Washington Place to live. But that's a long time ago.

Thirty-six years have passed since I came here a bride. My husband and his mother—both are dead. This is my home now. One flag alone flies over this domain. When various politicians suggest, ask, plead, even order me to raise another flag I tell them—

(To the politicians)

No, gentlemen. One flag alone flies here—our flag, the Hawaiian flag. My people must have somewhere to sing their songs and *mele*, somewhere to remember who they are; some bit of old Hawai'i to come back to. One flag, gentlemen, one flag.

(To the audience)

As I said, John brings me here a bride, and I am happy— except for the unhappiness around me. The Hawaiian people still mourning the little Prince's death, the King in seclusion, neglecting his official duties, threatening to abdicate; consoling himself by translating the Book of Common Prayer, and the Queen, numb herself with grief, trying to divert him.

As for the foreigners—well they are everywhere. Whaleships have been wintering in our waters for more than forty years. American missionaries have been our guests for the same length of time. Our streets are crowded with American businessmen, foreign diplomats, missionaries, ships' officers, and sometimes drunken sailors *(Sound of sea chanties)*—singing bawdy songs or lying in the gutter.

The businessmen talk of nothing but the declining

number of whalers in the harbor, and that depressing man in Pennsylvania—Coal Oil Johnny they call him— who's brought in a well that's producing finer quality, sweeter smelling, and cheaper oil than the oil the whalers bring. "Unless we find another industry," they cry, "our businesses will fail and grass will grow on Fort Street." Their one hope is sugar. Sugar. Fortunes can be made in sugar, they say, provided there's cheap labor and a duty-free market. This leads to open talk about coolies and contract labor and reciprocity with—even annexation to—the United States.

And we Hawaiians are asking, "How dare the foreigners talk of annexation—as though our islands are theirs to barter with—or give away—just so they get their labor cheap and their market duty free."

Soon after our wedding, Prince Lot invites John and me to join him and his party in a month-long tour of the Big Island. "Consider it your honeymoon," Lot says.

With the foreigners' possessive attitude toward our islands still haunting me, I see the island of Hawai'i, home of our fire goddess Pele, with new eyes.

(" 'Imi au iā 'oe," *or another song written during this period, underscores this speech*)

Impressive mountains and volcanoes, cool fern forests, deep valleys, abandoned *heiau*, velvety black lava flows where gnarled *'ōhi'a* flaunts its flame-red blossoms as though its very sap were living lava. As each day passes my love for my islands and for my people grows ever deeper and I celebrate my love in music.

(*An angry voice is heard offstage*)

KALA: *(To the audience)* That's Minister Cooper again. He's saying there are to be no singing and no speeches during the ceremonies. If anyone wants to sing or speak he may do so at the Opera House across the street—after the ceremonies.

LILI'UOKALANI: *(To the audience)* Our last night before we sail from Maui en route home, we stop at the beach home of friends of Prince Lot. The pig and sweet potatoes are in the *imu* and the ti leaves are gathered for the *lū'au*. I ask our host about his wife—why is she not here to welcome us?

"She hides," he says. Hides? "From the sheriff's men. She has the *ma'i Pākē*. The leprosy. They will take her from me if they find her. Send her to the receiving station in Honolulu."

A *lū'au* on the beach is usually a joyous occasion. Tonight we eat in silence. Halfway through the *lū'au*, darkness falls. Torches are lighted and a basket is placed before our host. Carefully, he wraps portions of the *lū'au* food in ti leaves until the basket's full. "For my wife," he says in a broken voice. "It's dark now, but the moon will rise." Then he stands up to leave, and my heart goes with him to the woman hiding out there in the darkness with her sickness.

Hours later he returns. The moon is up, the sea black gold and restless. John is sleeping off the *lū'au*, and ahead of me down the beach I see Prince Lot sitting cross-legged on the sand. He is wearing nothing but his *malo*. Lot is not the elegant Europeanized gentleman the King, his brother, has become. He is darker, heavier, more like his grandfather, the great Kamehameha. More like the chiefs of old before the strange ships came.

15

Prince Lot looks up as I approach. His eyes reflect the moonlight, but they are sad. Something in the look he gives me makes a lump form in my throat, grow big, and then break forth in one great sob as I drop to my knees beside him.

(Sound of ipu *and chanting)*
(To Prince Lot)

How did it happen, Lot? Our people sick and frightened, their bodies eaten by a disease that makes them hide—even from those who love them. Hide in caves and valleys while foreigners build their homes in choice places, walk our streets, and talk about new ways of making money.

Our *'āina,* which like the sea and sun and sky belongs to the gods, who lend it to each generation as it comes along, is now cut up in small parcels for men to buy and sell and haggle over and eventually end up in the possession of the foreigners for their children to inherit.

Ourselves, Lot? What's happening to us? Are we becoming merely imitation *haole,* speaking their language, eating their food, worshipping their God, wearing their clothes until we sweat and smell and then fall sick and die of their diseases?

I am afraid, Lot. Afraid the time will come when our men won't walk like chiefs, will not hold high their heads as they did in the days of their ancestors, afraid we will bow meekly, walk the foreigner's way, and not know who we are.

David Malo says that when the big wave rolls in, large fish come from the deep. When they see the other fish are small they gobble them up. Is the big wave rolling in, Lot? Are we being gobbled up?

(To the audience)

Prince Lot is on his feet, his dark eyes flashing. "If I were King," he cries, then stops. A man is running down the beach toward us. A messenger to tell Prince Lot he must come home at once, his brother the King is dying.

(Punchbowl guns)

A few days later the Punchbowl guns boom forth. The King is dead. Another gun salute, and heralds from the courthouse portico proclaim Prince Lot, King Kamehameha Fifth.

I can still hear his accession speech: *(Quoting portions of the accession speech)* "I am irreconcilably opposed to annexation. . . . Hawaiʻi will remain an independent sovereign nation, at peace with all. . . . Native customs will be revived. Royal powers and privileges will be restored. . . . We will bring in, not single male contract labor, but families of cognate races who will intermarry with our people, reinvigorate our ravaged population, and call Hawaiʻi home. . . . We cannot go back before the strangers came. . . . But from now on we can hold fast to who we are and what is ours. Hold fast! ʻOnipaʻa!"

He appoints my husband private secretary, confidential advisor, and governor of Oʻahu.

And I—I vow our people shall no longer rally to a borrowed anthem. They shall have one of their very own.

It is a stirring moment the following Sunday when the Stone Church choir *(choir singing one verse of "He Mele Lāhui Hawaiʻi")*, under my direction, stands up to sing. The atmosphere is tense. Everyone—Hawaiian and foreigner alike—knows what the King is thinking.

All goes well at first. But things are happening in the outside world of which we are now part. The American Civil War, with the North cut off from Southern sugar, is making Hawai'i's sugar a thriving industry, with most of the profits going into the foreigners' pockets. Sugar mills and sugar mansions are going up. Sugar planters are demanding—and getting—cheap labor. The cries for reciprocity—and annexation—become more frequent and more bold.

At one sugar planters' meeting a young man challenges the sugar planters: "The chief end of your meetings, gentlemen, is plantation profits. The burden of your cry is labor, cheap and immediate. But something far more important is at stake. Something fundamental is being ignored—the very future of the Hawaiian race."

The young man's name is Dole. Yes, Sanford B. Dole. The future leader of the men who bring about the downfall of the monarchy. The man who takes the reins of government from my hands. The man who signs my prison sentence and, eventually, my pardon.

(To Dole)

You see today how right you were, Mr. Dole. These beloved islands ours no longer. The Hawaiian people disinherited.

There was a time when you saw and protested what was being done to my people. You tried—not hard enough, it's true, but you did try—to stop the evil process. Even after you had joined the revolutionaries, after you became the *haole* counterpart of chief, you did sometimes befriend my people. You went to see those who feared they would be driven from the land I had leased to them, and you reassured them. And when those who tried and failed to return me to my throne were being sentenced to death or life imprisonment, you threatened to resign unless clemency were shown.

And yet—today you will arrive in your carriage at the rear gate of our Palace, you will be escorted to your seat on the roped-in platform, and at the proper moment you will stand and yield to a representative of the United States the sovereignty of our islands. And when the moment comes for the band to play "Hawai'i Pono'ī," you will be the one to give the signal for our flag to be hauled down forever. Forever. It will be nicely done, our flag will be folded carefully by loving hands, and put away somewhere forever—and everyone will be respectful and polite—as at a funeral.

(Sounds of the arrival of the Royal Hawaiian Band)

KALA: *(To the audience)* Captain Berger has just arrived. He is leading the members of the Royal Hawaiian Band to the spot where the halyards of the Hawaiian flag are tied.

LILI'UOKALANI: *(To the audience)* One evening when Prince Lot— the King, that is—is visiting with John I ask him when he is going to designate an heir. I tell him that if he doesn't do so, the legislature will designate one when he dies, and another royal prerogative will be lost.

As he hesitates one of those lovely fragile gold-white moths lights on the screen before us. Gradually, from the dark corners of the screen, they come—the geckos— until the moth's surrounded by them, radiating from it at the center like the spokes of a small wheel, their red tongues flicking in and out as they move closer. At last one pounces—

Of one accord we rise, and go outside, and as we walk along the moonlit beach we count the warships in our offshore waters, pointing toward our tiny kingdom.

Ships of France and Germany, Great Britain and Japan, Russia and the United States.

(Sounds of a drum corps arriving)

KALA: *(To the audience)* A drum corps has arrived. And a unit of the Citizens' Guard. They're taking their places near the roped-in platform. And now a platoon of fancy-uniformed policemen.

LILI'UOKALANI: *(To the audience)* In December 1872, seven chiefs and chiefesses are summoned to the Palace. The King is only forty-two but he is dying. With his death the Kamehameha line comes to an end. And there is no designated heir. We have gathered at his bedside. He looks at each of us in turn, then lets his eyes rest tenderly on the woman he had loved and hoped one day to marry—my *hānai* sister, Bernice Pauahi. "Will you?" he asks.

Bernice, married to a *haole*, feels she has forfeited the right to rule. "Why not your half sister, Princess Ruth?" she whispers.

Rebuffed again, he turns away. The small exertion is too much. Kamehameha Fifth is dead and we are king-less.

(Punchbowl guns)

As the Punchbowl guns announce his passing, a fear of crisis fills the room. Who will the American-dominated legislature select to rule us? One of the *ali'i*, yes, but which one? The two most likely candidates are standing together at the dead King's bedside: Prince William Lunalilo, first cousin to the dead King, beloved of the Hawaiian people, popular with the American element, and obviously unwell; and David Kalākaua, tall, hand-

20

some, deeply devoted to his people, and obviously in perfect health.

With a stab of pride and apprehension I realize that ours may one day be the ruling family, that my brother may be King.

An informal election shows our people overwhelmingly in favor of Prince William Lunalilo. When the legislature officially confirms their choice, and the Punchbowl guns announce the oath of office has been taken the kingdom, with a great sigh of relief, settles down. Now if Lunalilo will only designate an heir, the continuity of the monarchy will be assured and all will be well.

Within a year or so, however, King Lunalilo dies, and the legislature must once more elect our King. The two most favored candidates are my brother David Kalākaua, uncertain of his chances, and the beloved, romantic, doubly bereaved Queen Emma, who is confident she will be chosen.

On the day of the election, when David and I are awaiting the result, a woman—a *haole* woman—enters unannounced saying my brother has been elected. Others arrive to tell us that Queen Emma's supporters have smashed an arriving carriage, and are using pieces of it to force their way into the courthouse, belaboring the legislators and making angry accusations. I ask David—

(To David)

What do Emma's men mean, David—New York ward politics? Was your election a tug of war between British and American interests? Was it a case of gin and graft and bribery, as Emma's men are saying? Tell me, David —was it a clean fight? Would our ancestors approve? Does the torch that burns at midday still burn with a clean flame?

(To the audience)

My brother isn't listening. He is King now and he is consulting with advisors on what's to be done about the riot at the courthouse.

(Punchbowl guns)

Next morning early I go outside, and as I am walking barefoot in the grass, the Punchbowl guns announce the oath of office has been taken. As they speak again to designate our brother Leleiōhōkū heir apparent, it seems as though our grandfather, the High Chief Aikanaka, who in his time was guardian of the Punchbowl guns, is telling us once more the monarchy has been preserved, the Keawe-a-Heulu is the royal line, and Hawai'i's independence as a sovereign nation is assured.

The glittering accession ceremonies are barely over when I learn that David is making plans to go to Washington to lobby for the Reciprocity Treaty which will give the sugar planters their duty-free market. I am alarmed.

(To David)

Some of our people don't want the treaty, David. I know the foreigners want it. Yes, it will bring prosperity all right—but for whom? . . . Yes, and a lot of money—for the foreigners. It will bring other things, too. Shiploads of single males, who don't love our islands, who will work their contract time, then take their money and go home. The truth is, David, you are being used to get the treaty the foreigners wanted but couldn't get. Because the American government was afraid they would exploit our people. But if you, their Hawaiian King, ask for it, it will be granted. . . . You really think it will benefit our people? At first, perhaps, but in the end the large plantations will get larger and the small plantations will get smaller or be absorbed and what will happen to our people? . . . Yes, I know, David, you are King now, and what you say will come to pass. But there are those who say the Reciprocity Treaty will be the opening wedge by which our sovereignty is taken from us. Those of us who say it never should be signed.

(Sounds of carriages arriving)

KALA: *(To the audience)* The members of Mr. Dole's staff—in full uniform—have just arrived in their carriages. And Mr. Wilder—in full uniform—is conducting them to their reserved seats on the platform. Minister Cooper is instructing the drivers that the carriages must be securely tied some distance from the Palace, lest the guns alarm the horses.

LILI'UOKALANI: *(To the audience)* Kalākaua's trip to Washington is a triumphant tour. The people love him and he makes good copy for the reporters. He's taken to the circus in New York and becomes the main attraction. Eventually, the Reciprocity Treaty is signed, and the sugar planters get their market duty free.

Prince Leleiōhōkū, heir apparent, is regent in the King's absence. The foreigners like him. They comment on his polish and education and call him an asset to the dynasty.

Yet within two years he, too, is dying.

(Sound of ipu and funeral chant)

(To Leleiōhōkū)

Leleiōhōkū, why did you desert us? You, who personify the particular virtues of our race: love of life and beauty, talent for music and poetry, spontaneous gaiety, oneness with all of nature, and passionate attachment to the land. I know the doctors said pneumonia, but what do you say? Did you see the ugly story unfolding and did you choose to leave before the end? Did you shudder at the bitter rivalries developing between American and British, *haole* and Asian, Hawaiians and foreigners? Did it sicken you to see *aloha* turn to hatred, moonlight nights profaned by secret meetings where evil plots were being hatched? Did you prefer the company of your *'aumakua* to that of businessmen and politicians bent on power and profit till they would stop at nothing? Did it break your heart to see the strangers bring diseases that moved like raging fire to decimate our population—leaving one in ten alive?

Was it too much to bear, the realization that our open-hearted welcome of the stranger was becoming our undoing? *(Punchbowl guns)* I can still hear the Punchbowl guns, my brother, marking your departure. They speak again, to designate me, your sister, heir apparent in your place, under the title Lili'uokalani. *Aloha,* my dear brother, *aloha.*

(To the audience)

It is my conviction that the realization of what it would mean to be—as king—the tool of foreign interests, hastened my brother's death. He must have seen his brother David struggling frantically to extricate himself from the situation he'd fallen heir to. He must have wondered at the strange relationships and the wild schemes the King was driven to. He must have guessed where it would end.

But it isn't all dissension. There are good times in between.

KALA: *(To the audience)* Yes, there were good times in between. Band concerts when people came together in friendliness. Baby *lū'au* when new life was welcomed. Gay parties. Balls and lavish dinners for ships' officers and visiting diplomats. There was the coronation when the Keawe-a-Heulu line was officially installed. The planning and the building of the Palace. And the King's fiftieth birthday party—with prayers and pageants, and the Palace ablaze for the first time with the miracle of electric lights. And the grand ball afterward—the women in Paris gowns with trains and jewels. The men in uniforms complete with buttons and gold braid. Oh, it was beautiful—

LILI'UOKALANI: *(To the audience)* A beautiful charade. For underneath is fear, unrest, and bitterness on our part at being pushed aside by foreigners who now boast openly that though they are only five percent of the population they represent all of the culture and ninety percent of the wealth; who expect us not to mind when they smile indulgently at our *kāhili*, and our—our comic opera kingdom as they call it, when all the time they are coveting, to go with the wealth their sugar interests bring, the pomp and privilege of title, the best seats on state occasions, the uniform of office, not to mention complete control of the affairs of government.

The confrontation between Kalākaua and those of foreign blood comes when he is separated from those closest to him. His Queen and John and I are in London representing Hawai'i at Queen Victoria's golden jubilee.

We return to our hotel from Queen Victoria's farewell garden party to learn that in Hawai'i the unbelievable has happened. The foreigners, without appeal to suffrage, have forced the King—at bayonet point—to sign a constitution which deprives him of all power and practically disenfranchises two-thirds of our own people.

We cancel our planned tour of Europe and begin the long trip across two oceans home. We arrive midmorning on a hot day in July. The wharf is crowded with our people. The Royal Hawaiian Band serenades us. As I come down the gangplank I see the salt trace of tears on every upturned face. Waiting on the pier are four new cabinet ministers—all white.

It's two days before my brother comes to see me. In my heart I am blaming him, accusing him of weakness, of cowardice, but when I see his stricken face everything inside me melts.

(To Kalākaua)

How did it happen, Kunāne? How could it happen? Why did you sign their constitution? . . . Compelled you to? But you are King—who could compel you? . . . But your advisors? . . . Betrayed you? . . . Yes, John told me the hall was lined with soldiers with fixed bayonets. . . . But when you realized that the soldiers were not there to protect you but to coerce you, what did you do? . . . Yes, you had to choose. . . . But you could have chosen not to sign. . . . Yes, you could have chosen death.

(To the audience)

When my brother first tells me of threats against his life I only half believe him. Until the day a "mission boy" calls on me. He asks if I will consider becoming Queen in case my brother David is deposed. I listen patiently to what he has to say, then give him my answer.

(To the "mission boy")

As you know, I have been associated with missionary activities all my life. The innumerable requests—for time, money, work, sympathy, advice—have never gone unanswered.

I am familiar with the high and worthy purpose for which your parents were sent here by the American Board of Foreign Missions—to work for no private or worldly object but wholly for the good of others and the glory of God. To open your hearts wide, to aim at nothing short of covering the islands with fruitful fields and pleasant dwellings and schools and churches.

I believe, at first, those were your intentions. But sugar money has made some of you forget. Fruitful fields your Board of Missions said, not huge plantations yielding profits to yourselves. Pleasant dwellings for the many, they said, not sugar mansions for the few. Working for the good of others, not working for yourselves while you betray the native rulers. As for the political propaganda that issues from the very pulpit of the Stone Church—is that for the glory of God? No. You are betraying both your Board of Missions and your God—the God you have taught me to love. I have gone hand in hand with you in your works of good—and they are many. I will not join you in your works of evil. . . . I *have* given you my answer, sir. I will not join you in your works of evil. . . . Confidential? If you wish. I shall tell no one—except my diary and my King.

(To the audience)

When I tell my brother about the visit of the "mission boy," he looks at me in disbelief. "And they are telling me," he says, "that you are the *kipi* planning my overthrow."

(Commotion outside)

KALA: *(To the audience)* Marines—American marines—are lining up facing the roped-in platform and Minister Cooper is explaining that the American flag will be raised, not from the ground, but from the tower. Surely the P.G.s aren't worried for their safety; surely they aren't taking seriously certain rumors that are going round—that as our flag comes down a trap door will open and Mr. Dole and his cabinet ministers will disappear from sight for good? Is that why the unit of the National Guard and the fancy uniformed policemen?

LILI'UOKALANI: *(To the audience)* I know now, not only were there plans to dethrone my brother, there were plans to kill him. To hold a contest, and as he walks across an unprotected space to crown the winner, he will be shot. Lots are drawn to see which of these upright men will pull the trigger. At the last moment he loses courage—the one who drew the shortest straw.

Early in November 1890, David tells me he is leaving for the United States, partly on account of health, partly in connection with the McKinley Bill, passed by the American Congress, which has plunged the sugar interests into despair. I am to be regent in his absence. Abruptly, as he is talking, tears fill his eyes as he deplores the condition of the kingdom he is leaving in my care.

The royal guard, he says, has been reduced to twenty-five men. All arms have been removed from the

Palace grounds. Various factions are vying with each other to unnerve him—keeping the kingdom in constant turmoil. At last he smiles again as he recalls a group of Hawaiian men, in black suits, with top hats and gloves, marching to the Palace with a petition for a new constitution restoring to him his kingly powers and to themselves the right to vote. "Promise me," he says, "if I do not return, that you will work for these same ends, especially to return our people to their land." I promise. A quick embrace, and he is gone.

I hear the royal carriage leave the Palace. I hear the band salute him. The minute guns mark his departure. I think I knew it then—that he would not return; that the cares of office which had broken him would soon be mine.

(Sound of carriages arriving)

KALA: *(To the audience)* The carriages of the "important personages" are arriving.

LILI'UOKALANI: *(To the audience)* Months later, when it's time for David to return, I am awakened one morning early by a telephone call from the prime minister. He says the *Charleston*—the ship on which the King is to return—has been sighted by the lookout. I don't want to waken John—his rheumatism is acute. The prime minister calls again. The ship's yards are cockbilled and the entwined American and Hawaiian flags are at half mast. I order my carriage and drive to the Palace. As the horses turn into the Palace grounds I see two men wrapping cloth—black draperies—around the flower-covered arches raised to honor the King's return. I ask them why. They turn away to hide their tears.

Suddenly I understand. David isn't coming home.

David is dead. I am alone now, alone with my promise to return our people to their rightful place in these islands. To rule as a mother who puts the welfare of her children above all else, to replace the Bayonet Constitution with one more fair to all, and to help our people get back upon the land. And I—I am no longer heir apparent. No longer regent. I am Queen—Queen Lili'uokalani. As I promised David, I am ready.

INTERMISSION

(The sound of arriving carriages grows louder, and continues during the intermission and well into the second act)

"I've seen our flag hauled down before." *(Photo by Irwin Nakasone. Courtesy of Manoa Valley Theatre.)*

"Leleiōhōkū, why did you desert us?" *(Photo courtesy of Steven Michael's.)*

"The carriages of the 'important personages' are arriving." *(Photo courtesy of Steven Michael's.)*

"I live in sorrow, imprisoned."
(Photo by Irwin Nakasone.
Courtesy of Manoa Valley
Theatre.)

"We wait, suspended between hope
and fear." (Photo courtesy of Steven
Michael's.)

"The Queen paid no attention to the scandalous untruths, the shameless lies." *(Photo courtesy of Steven Michael's.)*

"But it isn't all dissension." *(Photo courtesy of Steven Michael's.)*

"Confidential? If you wish. I shall tell no one except my diary and my King." *(Photo courtesy of Steven Michael's.)*

"I was one of the young ladies educated by the Queen, so I know that statement for a lie." *(Photo courtesy of Steven Michael's.)*

"Behold not with malevolence / The sins of man, / But forgive and cleanse." *(Photo courtesy of Steven Michael's.)*

Act Two

(Minister Cooper's voice is heard above the sound of carriages)

KALA: *(To the audience)* Minister Cooper is saying he wants it to be understood that the Annexation Ball this evening is for everybody—everybody above nursery and kindergarten age—costumed within the category of democratic respectability. He is also repeating that the American flag will be raised, not from the ground, but from the central tower. Two smaller flags will be raised at the corners. This will take place as close to twelve noon as possible.

LILI'UOKALANI: *(To the audience)* My first impulse, on realizing that King Kalākaua is dead, is to return to Washington Place, to John, for comfort. But I am Queen now. My place is at the Palace.

My carriage pulls up to the entrance. I go immediately to the Blue Room. But I am not to have one moment to adjust to my new role. They are there before me, waiting, as they waited at the gangplank—the four cabinet ministers.

I greet them and sit down. In the silence I can hear them breathing. Suddenly there is a loud knock on the door and someone ushers in an officer from the *Charleston.* Looking straight at me, he says, "Admiral Brown wishes me to inform Your Majesty—the King is dead."

I see John in the doorway, come from his sickbed to be with me. I can still see his face, sharpened by his sickness, yet tender with concern for me.

Next thing I know I'm in the throne room, surrounded by a lot of men, including the cabinet ministers. The chief justice is telling me to repeat after him, "I solemnly swear in the presence of the Almighty God—" Suddenly I realize that it's the Bayonet Constitution that I am swearing to support. My voice falters. The words die in my throat. The cabinet ministers look at one another. The chief justice clears his throat.

John whispers, "Now is not the time to protest." I complete the oath.

(Punchbowl guns)

Minutes later the Punchbowl guns are booming and heralds on the street are crying, "Liliʻuokalani Queen! Long live Liliʻuokalani! Long live the Queen!"

I return to the Blue Room to receive condolences on my brother's death. Again they are there before me— the cabinet ministers. When the condolences are over, their first request of me as Queen is that I sign their commissions so that, as they put it, the business of government can go on uninterruptedly. I tell them—

(To the cabinet ministers)

But, gentlemen, I cannot appoint new cabinet ministers until you have resigned. . . . But your commissions ended with King Kalākaua's death. . . . I appreciate your concern that the government continue uninterruptedly. I assure you that it will. But you must first resign, so that new commissions may be signed. . . . Do I understand that you refuse? . . . Then I must refer the matter to the chief justice himself for a formal—public— ruling.

(To the audience)

Of course he has to rule that their commissions ended with my brother's death. Of course they must resign.

The night of my accession ball, as I am about to descend the Palace stairway, I pause a moment to observe the guests arriving. A group of foreigners crowds the doorway. Kitty, my companion, calls them the five percenters. "The new aristocrats," she whispers bitterly. "It's money now, not *mana*." "No!" I say with such vehemence that they all glance upward, puzzled, then go back to greeting one another.

I descend to the throne room to receive the homage of my citizens. There, among the first and seemingly the most anxious to display their loyalty to me, are several of the five percenters, including the little man who today boasts openly, "From the moment Lili'uokalani became Queen, we planned her overthrow. We have been waiting for this day for more than thirteen years."

Thirteen years ago, when the King was on his trip around the world, and I was regent, smallpox breaks out in Honolulu. I stop all transportation between the islands, forbid vessels to take on passengers, enforce strict quarantine, and thus confine the epidemic to O'ahu. Three hundred of my people die instead of thousands. But businessmen are inconvenienced and the cry goes up, "She puts the natives' lives before the business interests." That's what the little man holds against me. Today he will be seated there, among the "important personages," to watch our flag come down forever.

KALA: *(To the audience)* The carriage of Mr. Thurston has just pulled up at the rear gate of the Palace. He is in full uniform and Mr. Wilder—also in full uniform—is conducting him to his reserved seat on the platform.

LILI'UOKALANI: *(To the audience)* The day comes for me, as Queen, to give audience to the members of the diplomatic corps. They all extend the usual courtesies except the American minister, Mr. Stevens. He presumes to lecture me as though I am a child, urging me to acknowledge the supremacy of the legislature. He is telling me—and the entire diplomatic corps—that I am nothing but a puppet Queen.

I assume that he is merely tactless and wonder that a great country like the United States lets itself be represented by such an awkward minister. But when, in his public speeches, he speaks disparagingly of emperors and kings, of monarch-cursed and enslaved nations, and even makes local references that anger members of the House of Nobles, I realize he is not ignorant. He is deliberately planning to make trouble in the kingdom. As time passes he gives more evidence of his determination to make trouble—his constant association with those who favor annexation, his friendship with those who seem to look with favor on my overthrow, and his unpardonable rudeness in my presence. In short, he is deliberately doing everything he can to promote annexation.

KALA: *(To the audience)* The American minister was just an old man, really. Maybe a little senile. Talking loud, pounding with his cane.

LILI'UOKALANI: *(To the audience)* One of my first acts as Queen is to propose a constitutional convention so that the hated Bayonet Constitution may be replaced with one more fair to my people. Only to be told by members of the House of Representatives, "There is no money for a constitutional convention."

(To members of the House)

Why is there no money, gentlemen? You spend five thousand to send a delegation to Washington. Twelve thousand to send the Royal Hawaiian Band to the World's Fair in Chicago. Fifty thousand to repair the Volcano House road, but say there is no money to give my people what they are begging for—a new constitution. My desk's piled high with petitions. . . . But some of you gentlemen were elected on a promise to support such a convention. . . . Very well. If lack of money is your excuse, then other methods must be found. Other methods more direct.

(To the audience)

By now, it's clear to me, as I tell John,

(To John)

I am acting in good faith, the opposition is not. I am trying for a stable government—my enemies are not. I am trying to economize—I have cut my privy purse by ten thousand dollars, but they are spending money freely. They are doing everything they can to thwart me and weaken the government. And repeated lack-of-confidence votes against my cabinet appointments. What do they want? A cabinet committed to annexation to the United States? I am committed to the preservation of the prerogatives of the crown and to the independence of our islands.

(To the audience)

But John is grieving over his mother's death. He too is ill. He dies a few months later. I wonder—I can't help but wonder—if John had lived, if I had not been deprived of his support and counsel, could the overthrow have been averted?

I appeal to members of the House.

(To members of the House)

You and I, gentlemen, gave a promise to the Hawaiian people. All efforts to keep that promise are being blocked. We must, therefore, take a method more direct. It has always been the indisputable prerogative of the sovereign to proclaim a new constitution. I will draft a constitution in which the rights of all are regarded. At the proper time I will proclaim it. There is no other way. I have a promise to my people, and I must keep it.

(To the audience)

At noon on Saturday, the fourteenth of January, 1893, the household troops are lined up in front of the Palace. The band is playing. A procession of native Hawaiian men, in dark suits, top hats, and gloves, bearing a covered package, await my instructions. The covered package contains a copy of the new constitution, the one I will proclaim today in the throne room to invited guests and from the upper balcony to my beloved people. I am waiting in the Blue Room. At a special meeting earlier that morning I have asked my cabinet ministers to meet me here so we may go together to the throne room to proclaim the new constitution.

I am aware that anything may happen. But I am calm. Mr. Wilson, the marshal, and Captain Nowlein, of the household guards, both assure me they are ready to quell a riot if need be or an outbreak from the opposition. But my cabinet ministers are late—three-quarters of an hour late.

(To the ministers)

Come, gentlemen. My guests are waiting in the throne room. Come, sign the constitution. . . . But I don't understand. . . . But you agreed, you even urged me to proclaim this constitution today. You insisted now was the time. But you promised your support. . . . Afraid? Afraid of what? . . . Of an uprising from the opposition? Come, you see my people down there in the courtyard? My people, to whom these islands belong—by right of discovery, settlement, and centuries of living. By the bones of their ancestors buried here. It is from them that you should fear an uprising. They are tired of being disinherited. Tired of seeing their Queen humiliated. Come, gentlemen. . . . You what? . . . You have not read it? You, Mr. Peterson, have had it in your possession a month or more. You have consulted various lawyers on its provisions. Very well. If you insist you haven't read it, then take time now to read it. . . . Something wrong with it? . . . An unimportant detail— the legislature can make the necessary corrections. . . . You still refuse to sign it? Gentlemen, why didn't you tell me this morning? Why did you encourage me to invite the legislature, the diplomatic corps, the supreme court justice, and members of the Hui Kālai-ʻāina?

Are you traitors, gentlemen? Have you deliberately urged me to proclaim a constitution you had no intention of supporting? Or are you merely cowards? Come— one of you—sign it. Then I will go in there and proclaim it and take whatever happens.

(To the audience)

They still refuse to sign. At four o'clock I go into the throne room where my weary guests are waiting.

(To her weary guests)

Because the Bayonet Constitution is full of defects, and because I am told there is no money for a constitutional convention to remedy the defects, I have prepared a new one which I expected to proclaim today, in your presence. However, with deep regret I admit I have met with obstacles and must postpone it for a few days more. Therefore, with sorrow, I dismiss you.

(To the audience)

I leave the throne room and start upstairs, but when I reach the landing a commotion breaks out in the courtyard where my people have been waiting. From the upper balcony I tell them—

(To the people)

My loving people, I say to you, I was ready to proclaim the new constitution, thinking I would be successful, but behold, obstacles have arisen. Go with good hope and do not be troubled in your minds. Because I will proclaim the new constitution *ua kēia mau lā*. Return to your homes and keep the peace. I assure you of my love, and ask you to pray for me—as I pray for you.

(To the audience)

As I turn away, an angry voice rings out—

KALA: They have betrayed us!

LILIʻUOKALANI: *(To the audience)* One word from me at that moment, and my people would have taken things into their own hands. One word—but I tell them to return home peaceably—for I have been warned that a peaceful attitude must be maintained lest the United States send vessels of war to protect their citizens—and out of love for me they do.

(As cheers are heard outside)

KALA: *(To the audience)* Mr. Dole's carriage has arrived. Mr. Wilder is conducting him and Mrs. Dole to their seats on the roped-in platform.

(Discordant music)

LILIʻUOKALANI: *(To the audience)* Only when I am alone, the door closed tight behind me do I allow my heart to break. I watch the darkness gather and turn into night. I watch the brilliant moon ride high, and marvel that there is still beauty in the world for me.

Still I must not despair. I know that if it comes to open conflict, I can fight the revolutionaries with the forces at my command and win.

Sunday is a quiet day. Monday there are two mass meetings, one in the armory, consisting principally of the male white foreign element, and the other in Palace Square—including my supporters who love their chiefs and the traditional Hawaiian ways.

(Crowd sounds)

The mass meetings over, everything is quiet. It is a balmy evening, with people on the streets, men, women, and children converging on the Hawaiian Hotel *(Sounds of band tuning up)* where the band is getting ready for a concert. I am on the upstairs balcony of the Palace. Suddenly, off in the direction of the pier, I hear another kind of music—martial music—still indistinct and far away. Then the sound of men marching, coming closer, closer. Foreign troops do sometimes come ashore for practice, but for today no permission has been asked, none given. The marching men come closer till I can see them clearly. Suddenly, I realize—these are not peaceful troops ashore for practice. These are American sailors and marines and they are armed. Guns, double cartridge belts, Gatling guns, hospital corps, and stretchers. This is an act of war!

They reach the Palace and pause for a salute. Four ruffles on the drum. Four ruffles on the drum! I hear them now. I sometimes hear them in my sleep—I shall hear them when I am dying—four impertinent ruffles on the drum.

Suddenly my ministers arrive. Mr. Stevens, they say, has ordered troops ashore to protect the lives and interests of American citizens.

(To the ministers)

Protect them from what? Happy people strolling to a concert? And if indeed that is his purpose, why hasn't he ordered them inland—Makiki Heights, for instance—where the Americans and their interests are? Why are they lined up within a stone's throw of the Palace, their guns at ready? And if there is real danger, why aren't the other ships in harbor landing troops to protect their citizens?

(To the audience)

Dr. Trousseau arrives with his black bag. He brings a glass of water and offers me a pill.

(To Dr. Trousseau)

To quiet my nerves, Dr. Trousseau? This is armed invasion. This is war! With my own forces I can fight the revolutionaries and win. But what chance have I against armed troops of the United States?

(Band playing last of a song)
(To the audience)

Dr. Trousseau and my ministers leave. I am alone. The concert's over and the people have gone home to bed, completely unaware—as I am at the time—of a meeting in Nuʻuanu at which the revolutionaries are putting finishing touches on their plan to take what they have coveted all along—complete control of our beloved islands.

Somehow I get through the night. Darkness passes and the morning comes. My ministers, at my request, are gathered in the Blue Room. But we are barely assembled when there is a loud knock on the door and Mr. Walker enters. He is come, he says, on a painful mission. He represents the opposition. They suggest I abdicate.

Others arrive bringing news that half an hour earlier, in an all but empty government building, a proclamation has been read, a proclamation purporting to depose me, abrogate the monarchy, and set up a provisional government until terms of union with the United States can be agreed upon.

The man who read that proclamation came here from California, about two years ago. The all-but-empty government building in which he read the proclamation is but a few yards from the encamped American troops. The proclamation itself is a first-draft typescript dictated from the sickbed of the little man who now boasts of his determination to bring about my overthrow.

Within an hour of the reading of the proclamation, the American minister, with armed troops to back him up, has recognized the so-called provisional government.

KALA: *(To the audience)* Minister Cooper, who is policing today's ceremonies, is the man who read the proclamation abrogating the monarchy in the all-but-empty government building—recently arrived, of foreign birth. Excuse me. The carriage of the American Minister Sewall has just arrived at the rear gate and Mr. Wilder is conducting him to his reserved seat among the "important personages."

LILI'UOKALANI: *(To the audience)* I cannot bring myself to abdicate. These islands, entrusted to me for my people—suddenly a childhood memory comes back with startling vividness. The crowded Fort downtown, the King, eyes red from weeping, at the mercy of British guns, proclaiming to his people, "I cede these islands under protest, for I believe that when Queen Victoria learns the truth she will restore to us our sovereignty." Now, half a century later, almost to the day, I, at the mercy of American guns, will yield—under protest—not to the provisional government but to the United States, believing that when her statesmen know the truth they will restore to us our sovereignty, and once again the land will be preserved in righteousness.

At six o'clock I sign the protest. My next act is to write to the American president, Mr. Benjamin Harrison, giving my reasons—

(At her desk, speaking as she writes)

—for yielding to the superior force of the United States, the futility of conflict with your country, the desire to avoid violence and bloodshed, and the certainty that you and your government will right whatever wrongs have been inflicted upon us. In time a statement of the true facts will be laid before you. I pray that you will not allow any conclusion to be reached by you until my envoy arrives.

(To the audience)

I also write to President-elect Grover Cleveland.

(The sound of carriages arriving has stopped)

KALA: *(To the audience)* Apparently all the "important personages" have arrived. The rear gate to the Palace grounds is being closed and the two bandstands are being rearranged.

LILI'UOKALANI: *(To the audience)* I appoint Attorney Neumann to go to Washington on my behalf, but I am obliged to tell him—

(To Mr. Neumann)

The revolutionaries have chartered the only ship available and are refusing passage to my envoy. Your earliest chance is an Australian ship passing through en route to San Francisco within two weeks. This means the P.G. envoys will reach Washington before you even leave the islands.

(To the audience)

On February first, the day the revolutionaries' delegates are due in Washington, *(Punchbowl guns)* the city of Honolulu is shaken by a twenty-one-gun salute. As the American flag is raised above the Palace, heralds in the street announce that the American minister, John L. Stevens, is declaring Hawai'i an American protectorate. I now know that on that very day Mr. Stevens wrote his State Department, "The Hawaiian pear is now fully ripe and this is the golden hour for the United States to pluck it."

Next, the P.G.s order every government employee to sign an oath of allegiance. When all but sixteen members of the Royal Hawaiian Band refuse to sign, they are discharged. They form their own band *(Sounds of the band)*, and give their first concert here in my garden. From all directions my people gather, and when it comes time to sing *"Hawai'i Pono'ī"* even the heavens weep a little as every voice—including mine—joins in.

Next day the provisional government forbids the singing of *"Hawai'i Pono'ī"* without permission. And the threat is made that anyone failing to take the oath of allegiance will be forced "to eat stones."

Meanwhile we must stand by in horror as our Palace is denuded of the "trappings of royalty," as the P.G.s call them.

The P.G. envoys in Washington are telling their story of the overthrow, which includes the statement that "the overthrow was not in any way promoted by the United States. No troops or officers of the United States were present or took any part whatever in these proceedings." And here in Honolulu, Mr. Thurston, speaking as though the islands belong to him personally, threatens that if the treaty isn't ratified at once he'll give the islands to Great Britain.

The local and the American press are flooded with stories intended to justify the overthrow. Painting themselves as reasonable, determined, upright, cultured Christian leaders, they, in most un-Christian language, call my people blood-thirsty heathens and their Queen an idolatrous, half-mad creature of gross political and grosser personal immorality.

KALA: (*To the audience*) A Fresno editor wrote: "The Hawaiians have dethroned the fat squaw they have hitherto chosen to call Queen." But four days later the same editor wrote, "The more closely it is examined the more it looks like a deliberate scheme on the part of a band of schemers to deliberately create a crisis to precipitate annexation to the United States." And a little later, another editor: "Cleveland has withdrawn the treaty after discovering that it was the result of a plan formulated by the sugar-producing element, fathered in San Francisco."

The Queen paid—or appeared to pay—no attention to the scandalous untruths, the shameless lies, some so cruel that even the P.G.s chastised the authors. Each new outrage is accompanied by the P.G.s' protest, "We bear no ill will toward the natives themselves. For them we have nothing but *aloha*."

LILI'UOKALANI: *(To the audience)* When my envoy arrives in Washington, President Harrison has already sent the annexation treaty to the Senate, with a recommendation for prompt and favorable action. Undaunted, my envoy sets about correcting the story of the overthrow.

For me, there are long days and weeks of waiting, when rumors, threats, and insults are the order of the day, with nights of sudden noises and strange men lurking about these premises. Days of silence, of not knowing, of waiting for an end of waiting, until the body and the mind rebel, until one cannot think or feel, and even *poi* turns rancid in one's mouth.

Then at last one day the editor of a friendly newspaper telephones, and I give Kitty the good news—

(To Kitty)

Oh, Kitty, President Cleveland has withdrawn the annexation treaty from the Senate. He is sending Commissioner Blount to conduct an investigation.

(To the audience)

Commissioner Blount arrives. He rejects all offers of hospitality, hires a hack, and drives straight to the Hawaiian Hotel. His first act is to send the armed American troops back to their ship. *(Punchbowl guns)* Then he revokes the order making Hawai'i an American protectorate, and orders the American flag lowered, and the Hawaiian flag run up.

Naturally my people—hundreds of them—gather in the Palace grounds to stand silent and respectful as the

American flag comes down, silent and respectful as the Hawaiian flag is raised. Commissioner Blount is puzzled. Why are there no shouts of joy? The P.G.s tell him it's because the Hawaiians are indifferent. Don't care which flag flies over them. Later, when I have a chance to speak with him I tell him—

(To Commissioner Blount)

My people were not indifferent when the American flag was lowered, nor were they indifferent when their own flag was raised. They simply did not want to dishonor someone else's flag knowing how they love their own. Those gentle, silent people are the blood-thirsty savages the P.G.s have been telling you about.

(To the audience)

One day—quite unexpectedly—Commissioner Blount calls on me. He hands me a clipping from the *Star*.

(To Mr. Blount)

Commissioner Blount, we both know this is a lie.

(To the audience)

Immediately Commissioner Blount is all business. He sits down facing me and begins asking questions. Can I give him a written report of the overthrow? Yes. Am I afraid for my own safety? Yes, with Mr. Thurston saying he favors bringing things to a smash—by force if necessary. Can I tell him who the revolutionaries are? There are thirteen—nine American-born or island-born of American parents, two Germans, one Tasmanian, and one Scotsman. No Hawaiians. That's right—no Hawaiians. . . . The names of the revolutionaries?

I give them to him—one by one.

For four long months Commissioner Blount receives those willing to come forward, either in person or in writing.

Attempts are made to blacken everything I have said or done.

KALA: *(To the audience)* The P.G.s even said the marshal of the kingdom, Kitty's husband, was Her Majesty's paramour, and that the Queen's societies for educating young Hawaiian women were conducted really for immoral purposes. I was one of the young ladies educated by the Queen, so I know that statement for a lie. And when the Queen divided some of the crown lands into ten-acre plots and rented them to her people for one dollar a year, the P.G.s called this "reheathenizing the heathens." The land they said should be made the property of the government and put up for sale.

LILI'UOKALANI: *(To the audience)* At last, Commissioner Blount leaves for Washington with his report. My people bid him *aloha* with songs and flower *lei.* The P.G. band, however, marks the departure of this former officer of the Confederate Army with a spirited rendition of "Marching through Georgia."

We wait, suspended between hope and fear. Nights when dark figures prowl the shadows of my garden, when sudden bursts of gunfire disturb my rest. Days filled with insults, rumors, and threats against my life. Spies on the steps of the church across the street.

At last word comes. Commissioner Blount's report has been delivered to President Cleveland with these words: "The Hawaiians are overwhelmingly against annexation. We cannot condone a selfish and dishonorable scheme of adventurers. The Queen's submission was coerced."

And President Cleveland's response: "The Provisional Government owes its existence to armed invasion by the United States. My concern is to undo the wrong done by those men representing the United States. A feeble but friendly nation is in danger of being robbed of its independence. This calls for an investigation. I am sending Congressman Albert B. Willis to Hawai'i with a message for the Queen."

When Mr. Willis arrives, November 4, 1893, he immediately asks me to call on him at his hotel. Friendly advisors feel that this is unbecoming and suggest that I refuse.

(To her friendly advisors)

Has it occurred to you to wonder why he is hesitant to call on me? Have you forgotten the editorials in the P.G. newspapers: "If the Queen is restored she will never live a day"; "If Cleveland tries to restore her she will be murdered in cold blood." Have you forgotten the spies on the church steps? It may be for my protection—and his own—that he does not call on me. I will call on him as he requests. I do it for my people.

(To the audience)

Besides, I have a personal message for Mr. Willis. I will tell him of the treachery of my cabinet ministers while I was waiting for them in the Blue Room.

I am sitting on the sofa in the parlor of his quarters when he enters. He greets me warmly, then takes a straight-back chair and sits down facing me. He tells me that President Cleveland has come to the conclusion that the provisional government was not established by the Hawaiian people or with their consent and that he—President Cleveland—is prepared to do anything in his power to undo the wrongs—to restore me to the throne. Then, regarding me very closely, he asks, "Will you sign a proclamation giving complete pardon and protection for all those who were involved in the revolution?"

I hesitate. I know there will be no peace in our kingdom if some of the revolutionaries remain. I also know that no proclamation of mine will be binding without the signature of my ministers. I also know our law requires that those guilty of treason suffer the penalty of death. Would I insist on that? I personally would favor banishment, but I must talk it over with my privy council. There are those who claim that I said the revolutionaries should be beheaded. However much they may have deserved it, I never used those words.

A few days later, at my request, Mr. Willis calls on me here.

(To Mr. Willis, handing him a document)

I have consulted my conscience and my trusted friends. I have decided that I must forgive the past. I must think only of my people and my islands. Here, in writing, Mr. Willis, is my official reply to President Cleveland. I grant full amnesty to all who participated in my overthrow.

(To the audience)

Congressman Willis thanks me and says he will now call upon the provisional government, tell them of President Cleveland's decision and my grant of amnesty and ask them to abide by the president's decision.

But when he does the provisional government replies: "We are now an independent state. If Mr. Stevens and American troops acted illegally, that is a matter for the American conscience, not ours. We do not grant the president of the United States the right to meddle in our domestic policies. We decline to entertain the proposition that we surrender our authority to the ex-queen. Any attempt to make us do so will be resisted with armed force."

On December 18th, President Cleveland tells Congress the conditions on which he tried to restore the Queen, after which he turns the matter over to the Committee on Foreign Relations. He calls the landing of the troops "an act of war," and says further:

"The lawful government of Hawai'i was overthrown . . . by a process . . . directly traceable to . . . the agency of the United States acting through its diplomatic and naval representatives.

"But for the notorious predilections of the United States minister for annexation, the committee of safety, which should be called the committee of annexation, would have never existed.

"But for the landing of the United States forces upon false pretexts . . . the committee would never have exposed themselves to the pains and penalties of treason by undertaking the subversion of the Queen's government.

"But for the presence of the United States forces in the immediate vicinity the committee would not have proclaimed the Provisional Government. . . .

"But for Minister Stevens' recognition of the Provisional Government . . . the Queen would never have yielded. . . .

" . . . I shall not again submit the treaty of annexation to the Senate for its consideration, and in the

instructions to Minister Willis . . . I have directed him
to so inform the Provisional Government.

"But in the present instance our duty does not . . .
end with refusing to consummate this questionable
transaction. . . .

" . . . the government of a feeble but friendly and
confiding people has been overthrown. A substantial
wrong has thus been done which a due regard for our
national character as well as the rights of the injured
people requires we should endeavor to repair."

However, President Cleveland cannot act without
the support of Congress. Late in August we receive
word that President Cleveland has officially recognized
the Republic of Hawaii.

We must now face reality—no outside help will save
Hawai'i as an independent kingdom. You know what
happens next. My people, under the leadership of Captain Nowlein, decide to save their islands and restore
their Queen. When Captain Nowlein comes with others
to see me—here in this room—to ask, not for my
involvement but for my approval, I tell them—

(To her people)

Until now you have been peaceful out of respect for me.
You have patiently endured many wrongs, but, if at last,
you rise en masse determined to throw off the foreigners'
yoke, I will not say one word against it.

(To the audience)

They speak softly. "We will restore our Queen," they say.
Then they draw close and chant something I have never
heard before, about the stone eaters, who will not swear
allegiance—

60

(Chanting)

KALA:

Famous are the children of Hawai'i
Ever loyal to the land.

LILI'UOKALANI:

Kaulana na pua a'o Hawai'i
Kūpa'a mahope o ka 'āina.

KALA:

We do not value
The government's sums of money.

LILI'UOKALANI:

'A'ole mākou a'e minamina
I ka pu'u kālā a ke aupuni.

KALA:

We are satisfied with the stones,
Astonishing food of the land.

LILI'UOKALANI:

Ua lawa mākou i ka pōhaku,
I ka 'ai kamaha'o o ka 'āina.

(To the audience)

About four months go by, then on a Sunday evening, Captain Nowlein comes to see me. It must be a few minutes after eight, for evening services are just beginning in the church next door.

Captain Nowlein tells me everything is in readiness. He does not know—nor do I—that two hours earlier a spy has telephoned authorities that natives are assembling at the Bertleman place on Diamond Head, that a dozen policemen are on their way there, that roadblocks are being set up, and that—at that very moment—authorities are telephoning the pastor of the church.

Captain Nowlein leaves. I get my Book of Common Prayer and sit here by the light. Suddenly there is a strange commotion in the churchyard—people running from the church, women and children toward their carriages, the men toward the Armory. My prayer book slips from my hand, slides to the floor. The church is dark now and the sound of carriages has stopped. We have been betrayed again, and there is nothing I can do but wait. I go into my bedroom, undress, put on my blue flannel nightgown, and get into bed. Then all is silence except for the low talk of my guards.

The next morning everything is quiet in the city, but soon we learn that artillery in Kapiʻolani Park and cannon from an offshore tugboat are shelling the Hawaiians on the slopes of Diamond Head. Higher and higher they climb to avoid the shells, then move down into the valleys behind the city.

In the following ten days one hundred ninety-one are taken prisoner.

KALA: *(To the audience)* The flag-raising ceremonies are beginning. Everyone is standing. The men have removed their hats. Mr. Pearson is about to offer prayer.

LILIʻUOKALANI: *(To the audience)* The morning of January sixteenth, about ten o'clock, as I am resting in my room, Mrs. Clark comes in to tell me that Deputy Sheriff Brown and Captain Parker wish to see me. I tidy my hair and come into this room. Deputy Sheriff Brown, waving a white paper, tells Mrs. Clark and me to come with him. I assume we're going to police headquarters for questioning. When I reach the open doorway I see two hacks awaiting us. Captain Parker gets into the first and sits beside the driver. Then I get in and sit down in the back. The deputy sheriff takes his seat beside me. Mrs. Clark is in the second hack.

The two hacks drive rapidly to the Palace, enter by the Richards Street gate and draw up at the rear door. As I said, I was assuming we were going to police headquarters for questioning, but when I see the muzzles of brass field pieces pointing straight in our direction, when I see the military tents and soldiers and stacked guns—then I know I am a prisoner. Between the deputy sheriff and Captain Brown I climb the iron steps, walk along the hallway to the foot of the wide stairway leading to the upstairs of the Palace.

Colonel Fisher then takes charge—leads us up the majestic stairway. I pause a moment on the second floor landing as I face a life-size portrait of myself as Queen. Doors behind me open and I am conscious of curious foreigners observing every move I make. I check the rush of memories, the flood of anger and sorrow for my people and my islands, stand a little straighter, and move on. At last we are ushered into a room in my own Palace that I do not even recognize. Bare, uncarpeted, a single bed in the far corner, shutters closed and curtains drawn. Presently Colonel Fisher excuses himself. The door is closed and locked. We are alone.

The first night is the worst. Cut off from everything I love, I cannot see the sky, the clouds, the moon and stars. I cannot hear the birds. I cannot feel the trade winds on my cheek. I cannot tell when darkness falls or when the morning breaks. I cannot reach out to my people or feel their love. All I can hear are the footsteps of the sentry, pacing back and forth outside my door. And from the adjoining room the mournful sighs of Mrs.

Clark, worrying about her children. In the morning I'll send her home, ask Kitty to come in her stead.

KALA: *(To the audience)* I learn of the Queen's arrest from a P.G. newspaper: "A corporal guard stands watch over her. She is taken. Lili'uokalani Dominis is a prisoner. She is now wholly within the power of the provisional government. When she was arrested this morning, she did not faint, or cry out, or start back, or give any evidence of weakness. She was dressed entirely in black, carried no baggage—only a small white handkerchief."

LILI'UOKALANI: *(To the audience)* On the sixth day of my imprisonment I am presented with a formal abdication, for me to sign—written not by me but by paid attorneys hired by the men in power. In most abject terms I must declare the monarchy forever ended, absolve my people from allegiance to myself, renounce all claims upon the throne, implore clemency for my misguided people, and swear allegiance to the Republic of Hawaii.

It closes with the statement that I have written it "without the slightest suggestion from any member or official of the government."

Why do I sign that shameful document? Because I am told that unless I do a stream of blood will flow. Six of the Hawaiian leaders will be shot; others will be confined for long terms up to life; and heavy fines will be imposed. But if I sign, they promise, all those in trouble because of their love and loyalty to me will be released immediately.

The trials begin as though no promise of clemency had been given. Not one life is saved by my abdication; not one prisoner released; not one sentence commuted; not one human being rescued from the tanks of ice

64

water or slow starvation. It was a threat from the United States that saved those condemned to die—word that if anyone were executed the Republic of Hawaii need not hope for annexation.

Sometimes I ask myself, "Should I have refused to sign the abdication papers? Should I have let them kill me if they dared? Should I have let my faithful retainers die for their beloved islands?" There are things worth dying for. As the old chant says, "The land is the only living thing. Men are mortal. The land is the mother that never dies."

KALA: (*To the audience*) After the Queen signed the abdication, a violent earthquake shook these islands.

(*Sound of drums*)

LILI'UOKALANI: (*To the audience*) One hundred ninety-one prisoners come to trial before the military tribunal of the Republic of Hawaii. Even now I cannot bear to think of what the others suffered. Compared to their imprisonment, mine is little more than inconvenience. My meals are brought from my own kitchen, and eventually I am allowed visits from my doctor. Newspapers and the like are forbidden me, but I am allowed blank paper and a pencil, so my musical composition continues in the long quiet hours.

(LILI'UOKALANI *sings to an autoharp a verse of "The Queen's Prayer"*)

KALA: (*To the audience*) Mr. Dole and the American Minister Sewall have risen to their feet. Minister Sewall is handing Mr. Dole a document.

LILIʻUOKALANI: *(To the audience)* The *haole* leaders of the counter-revolution are tried first. All are found guilty, sentenced to be shot, and fined ten thousand dollars. The Hawaiians are tried in batches of twenty-five or more. Most are found guilty, sentenced to terms in prison, and fined.

I am tried last—not for treason, but for misprision—knowing about plans for the counterrevolution but not reporting it to the authorities. When Marshal Wilson comes for my written defense, which is to be read at the trial, he tells me, with great satisfaction, that I will not have to attend the trial.

(To Marshal Wilson)

But why not? . . . Too humiliating? . . . For whom? . . . For me? But they cannot humiliate me. My only humiliation comes if I fail my people. It is for my people that I endure. . . . For them I would spend everything belonging to me. For them I would give my last drop of blood. You cannot excuse me from my trial. I insist on being present.

(To the audience)

On the morning of February 8, 1895, accompanied by Kitty, I am escorted to my former throne room. *(Crowd sounds)* It is crowded with men of the diplomatic corps, ministers of the gospel, ships' officers, businessmen, women prominent in Honolulu social circles, citizens of every race—except Hawaiians. There are also soldiers with fixed bayonets. At a large table in the center of the room sits the military tribunal.

One friendly pair of eyes meets mine. American Congressman Willis stands up to warn the tribunal,

"The world is watching, gentlemen. You had best act with justice, not revenge."

Mr. Judd is the only witness against me. His only evidence, a sentence from my diary—"Signed eleven new commissions today"—which he says is proof that I had knowledge of the plot.

Attorney Neumann reads my statement, in which I describe my efforts to obtain a fair constitution, and how my enemies use this as a pretext for overthrowing the monarchy, and, aided by the United States naval forces and minister, establish the provisional government.

As he reads the rest of my statement, my heartbeat accents every word:

"I owe no allegiance to the provisional government, nor to any other power save the will of my people.

"I deny your right to try me by this court.

"I defend my right to appoint new cabinet members in anticipation of a possible restoration.

"There may be in your conscience a warrant for your actions but you can find no such warrant in any civilized Christian nation in the world. You, gentlemen, are on trial before the civilized world, with the happiness and prosperity of Hawai'i in your hands. May Divine Providence grant you the wisdom to lead the nation into paths of forbearance and forgiveness.

"As for my people whom you now hold prisoner—as you deal with them, so I pray may the Almighty God deal with you in your hour of trial."

Three weeks later I am summoned once more before the tribunal. Verdict: Guilty. Sentence: Five years at hard labor. Fine: Five thousand dollars.

Mr. Wilson returns me to my room. I never will forget the way it looked that day. Bare, uncarpeted, and yet, a guitar and autoharp are waiting for me on the table beside my unfinished sheet of music, a potted fern trembles on the window sill, two canary birds are chirping merrily, my *lau hala* fan laced with maidenhair fern is lying on the floor, and Kitty is standing in the middle of the room weeping.

KALA: *(To the audience)* Kitty told me that the Queen put her arm around her and let her weep a little on her shoulder, then whispered, "I'm not going to be deported. Or shot at sunrise."

LILI'UOKALANI: *(To the audience)* The months go by. Confinement begins to tell on me. I am permitted to walk—between armed guards—on the balcony in the evening after sunset. Then abruptly, on September 6 I am told to be ready for release under parole.

Can you imagine what it means to me to see my garden? My beloved tree ferns waiting silently, my orchids smiling at me, my violets asking to be picked. And a huge bunch of leathery red bananas ripe and ready for the eating. I touch them to be sure they're real. Then come my friends, aching to make me feel at home and loved.

And then this room—with all its memories. My handsome grand piano, gift of ardent music lovers; my desk, the little drawer where I kept my husband's jewelry. It's empty now—no, not quite. They've left a tiny bit of John—a collar button—gold.

Five months later, parole is lifted, but still I cannot leave the islands. Eight months later—in October—as I am standing in my garden, ready to replant some ferns, a government official hands me a piece of paper, signed by Mr. Dole. I am free, without restriction. Pardoned absolutely and my civil rights restored.

On December 5th I board the boat for San Francisco. "Christmas in Boston, with John's relatives," I tell my friends—which is true. But after Christmas, I'm in Washington when the P.G. annexation treaty is introduced once more in Congress. I protest the treaty:

Because it was before the force of the United States that I yielded my authority.

Because the president of the United States has admitted I was unlawfully coerced.

Because my people, forty thousand of them, have never been consulted by the three thousand who claim the right to destroy the independence of Hawai'i.

Because no authority has been given by the registered voters of Hawai'i.

Because the treaty ignores the hereditary property rights of my people.

Because the United States receives territories from those it has declared fraudulently in power.

Because we have relied for years on the protection of the United States. Will they withdraw it now?

Because our form of government is as dear to us as theirs is to them.

Because we love our country and our way of life as warmly as they love theirs.

Because the people to whom their fathers told of the living God are crying out to that God now, begging Him to hear the voices of his Hawaiian children lamenting for their homes.

The annexation treaty is defeated in the 1897 Congress. There is still hope. I stay on in Washington. But on the sixth day of July 1898 the Newlands Resolution passes. The next day President McKinley signs it into law. The beloved islands—blood of my blood, bone of my bones—are ours no longer. And ex-President Grover

Cleveland says publicly, "Hawai'i is ours, but as I contemplate the means used to complete this outrage, I am ashamed. Ashamed of the whole affair."

Ten days ago, I return to my people and my beloved islands. It's past midnight when we dock—dark and silent as I come down the gangplank. But I can sense them—out there in the darkness—my people. What can I say to them?

(In a firm voice)

Aloha kākou no kou kūpa'a.

KALA: *(To the QUEEN)* *'Ae aloha nō.*

LILI'UOKALANI: *(To the audience)* Suddenly the darkness comes alive. With flaming torch and chant and *mele* my people bring me here, to Washington Place, and seat me in this chair. One by one they pass before me. I call them each by name and wipe away the tears, sometimes from their eyes, sometimes from my own. And we know there is a land where no foreigners can come, where I am Queen, in the hearts of my people.

(Gun salute)

KALA: *(To the audience)* Soldiers are advancing to where the halyards of our beloved flag are tied. Mr. Dole is motioning to Mr. Soper and Mr. Soper is signaling to Captain Berger—

(A burst of music as the band plays "Hawai'i Pono'ī")

—but the Hawaiian musicians are throwing down their instruments and disappearing round the corner of the

Palace—to mourn in private, as our flag comes down forever.

(LILI‘UOKALANI *stands transfixed until* "Hawai‘i Pono‘ī" *comes to an end*)

LILI‘UOKALANI:
Beloved flag, *aloha.*

("Taps" is played)

Who will give us back our face?

(The strident sound of a bugle is followed by a gun salute, and the American ship's band playing the American anthem as the lights come slowly down)

END

About the Author

Aldyth Morris, born in the Rocky Mountain town of Logan, Utah, has spent most of her life in the Hawaiian Islands. She has written several radio plays and eight full-length plays. Among her best-known works set in Hawai'i are *Captain Cook, Robert Louis Stevenson,* and *Damien,* a Peabody Award winning monodrama also produced on videotape.

Mrs. Morris was managing editor of the University of Hawaii Press for fifteen years and editor of the East-West Center Press for two years.